There's nothing "new" in this book.

What's new is how fast your company can be transformed to dramatically unleash your brand's potential.

Brand Intervention showed you how to successfully build a brand by looking where others weren't and seeing what others didn't—and leveraging those insights—to eliminate that "sea of sameness" so many brands drown in.

Rich Brand Poor Brand takes it further, helping you craft a culture capable of sustaining the brand you've built.

> Culture is created by people.

The culture your brand builds needs to thrive on ideas and

communities to create the kind of environment that enjoys ingenuity for breakfast, inspiration for dinner, and courage for dessert.

This is all about unleashing your David in a world of Goliaths.

David had a slingshot and kicked Goliath's ass.

How?

By what he had? No.

He was smaller.
He had fewer resources.
He was less muscular.

Yet his success was based on the strongest weapon others underestimated: his ingenuity.

It was David's ingenuity that opened the eyes of those

around him, and opened the doors of opportunity to achieve what nobody thought was possible.

You can do the same.

It is ingenuity driven by keen insight that makes us infinitely stronger, more resilient, and insanely resourceful.

It also allows us to forge formidable alliances, leverage assets you won't find on a balance sheet, and build remarkable synergies—
the kind of synergies that impact our bottom line, maximize our impact in the world, and outsmart the Goliaths of the world.

All so our genius explodes and multiplies exponentially

as we unleash our David in a world of Goliaths.

Other than that, there's nothing new here.

So, grab a coffee.

Put your slingshot aside, and enjoy.

"Life shrinks or expands in proportion to one's courage."

Anais Nin

RICH BRAND POOR BRAND
How to Unleash Your David in a World of Goliaths

© 2024 David Brier. All Rights Reserved.

The information included in this book is based on the experience, observations, and conclusions of the author and the author's clients. It is provided here as anecdotal and informational. Although the author and publisher have made every effort to ensure that the information in this book was correct at press time, the author and publisher do not assume and hereby disclaim any liability to any party for any loss, damage, or disruption caused by interpretations, errors, or omissions of the material, whether such errors or omissions result from negligence, accident, or any other cause.

No part of this book may be reproduced or transmitted in any form or by any means, electronic or mechanical, including photocopying, recording, or by any information storage and retrieval system without written permission of the author and/or publisher.

Visit the author's website at **RisingAboveTheNoise.com** and **RichBrandPoorBrand.com** for new updates and Rich Brand Poor Brand exclusives.

ISBN 978-0-9995297-3-7 (Hardcover)
ISBN 978-0-9995297-4-4 (Paperback)
ISBN 978-0-9995297-5-1 (E-book)

Publisher: DBD International, Ltd.

Author/Designer: David Brier

Editor: Patricia Ross

Interior Layout: Ronda Taylor

All designs enclosed are the work of David Brier and/or DBD International, Ltd. and are the property of the respective companies they represent.

THE RICH BRAND

THE POOR BRAND

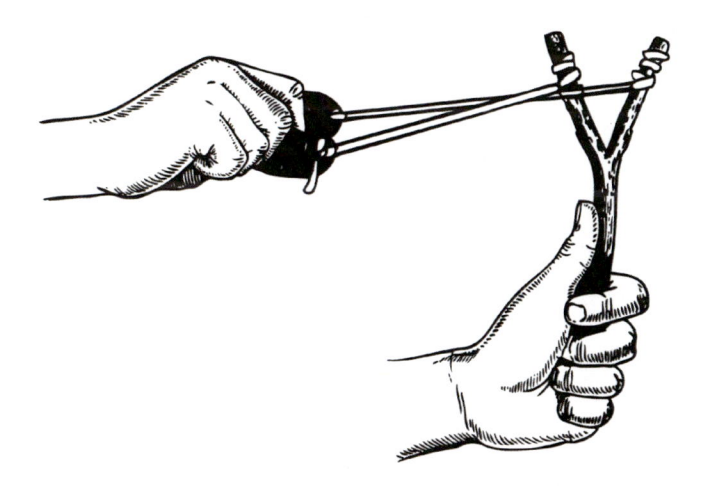

HOW TO UNLEASH YOUR DAVID IN A WORLD OF GOLIATHS

DAVID BRIER

FOREWORD by Claude Silver

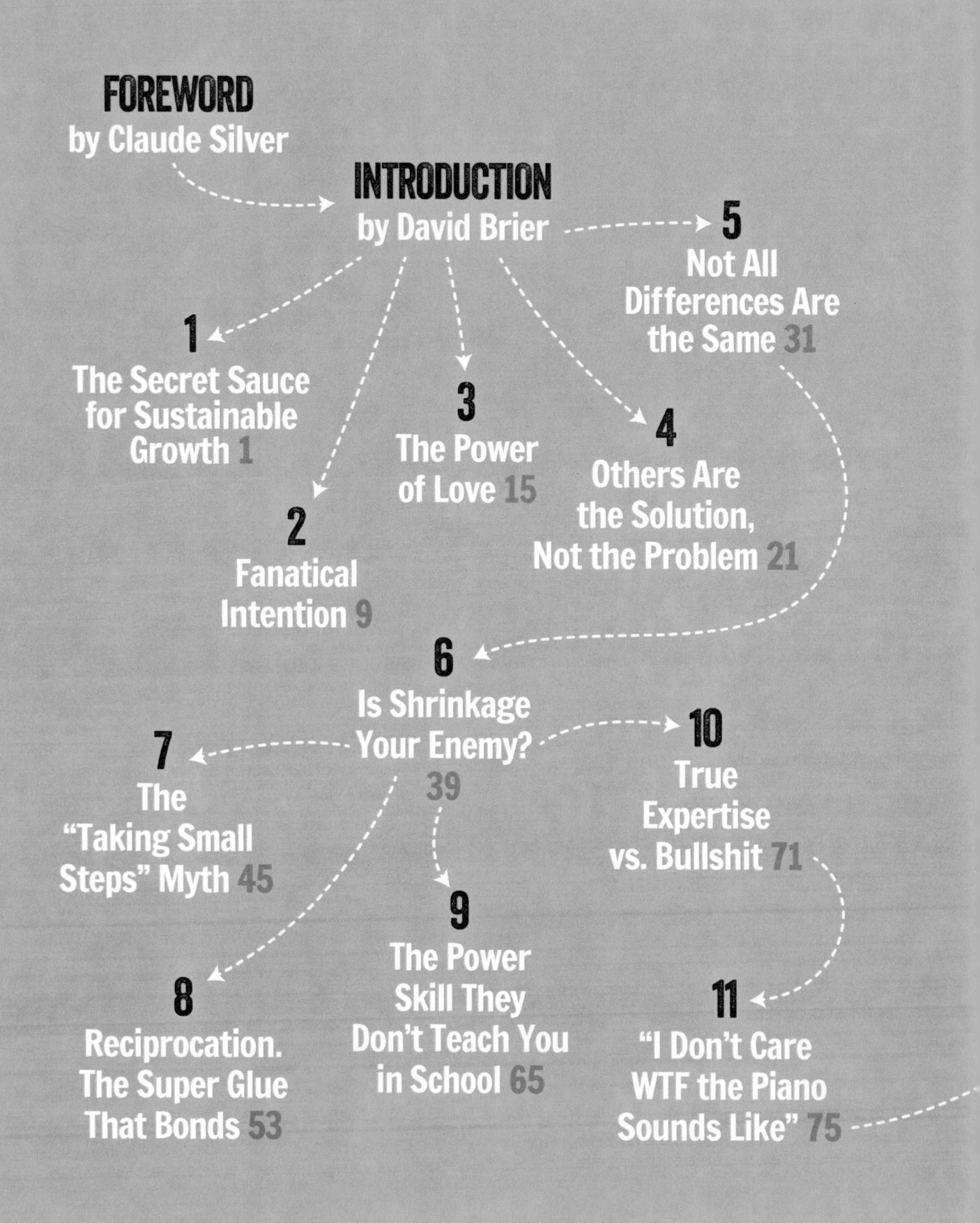

INTRODUCTION by David Brier

1 The Secret Sauce for Sustainable Growth 1

2 Fanatical Intention 9

3 The Power of Love 15

4 Others Are the Solution, Not the Problem 21

5 Not All Differences Are the Same 31

6 Is Shrinkage Your Enemy? 39

7 The "Taking Small Steps" Myth 45

8 Reciprocation. The Super Glue That Bonds 53

9 The Power Skill They Don't Teach You in School 65

10 True Expertise vs. Bullshit 71

11 "I Don't Care WTF the Piano Sounds Like" 75

12 The Smartest Answer: "I Don't Know" 85

13 78 Balloons: A Lesson in Teamwork 93

14 The Lifeblood of a Team 101

15 Ideas Have Direction 111

16 The 3-30-3 Rule 117

17 How to See Around Corners 127

18 The Law of Expansion 135

19 The Kind of Comfort That Kills Teams and Brands 139

20 Creating a Company of Giants 145

21 How to Unleash Your David in a World of Goliaths 153

PLAYBOOK 167

LAST WORD 205

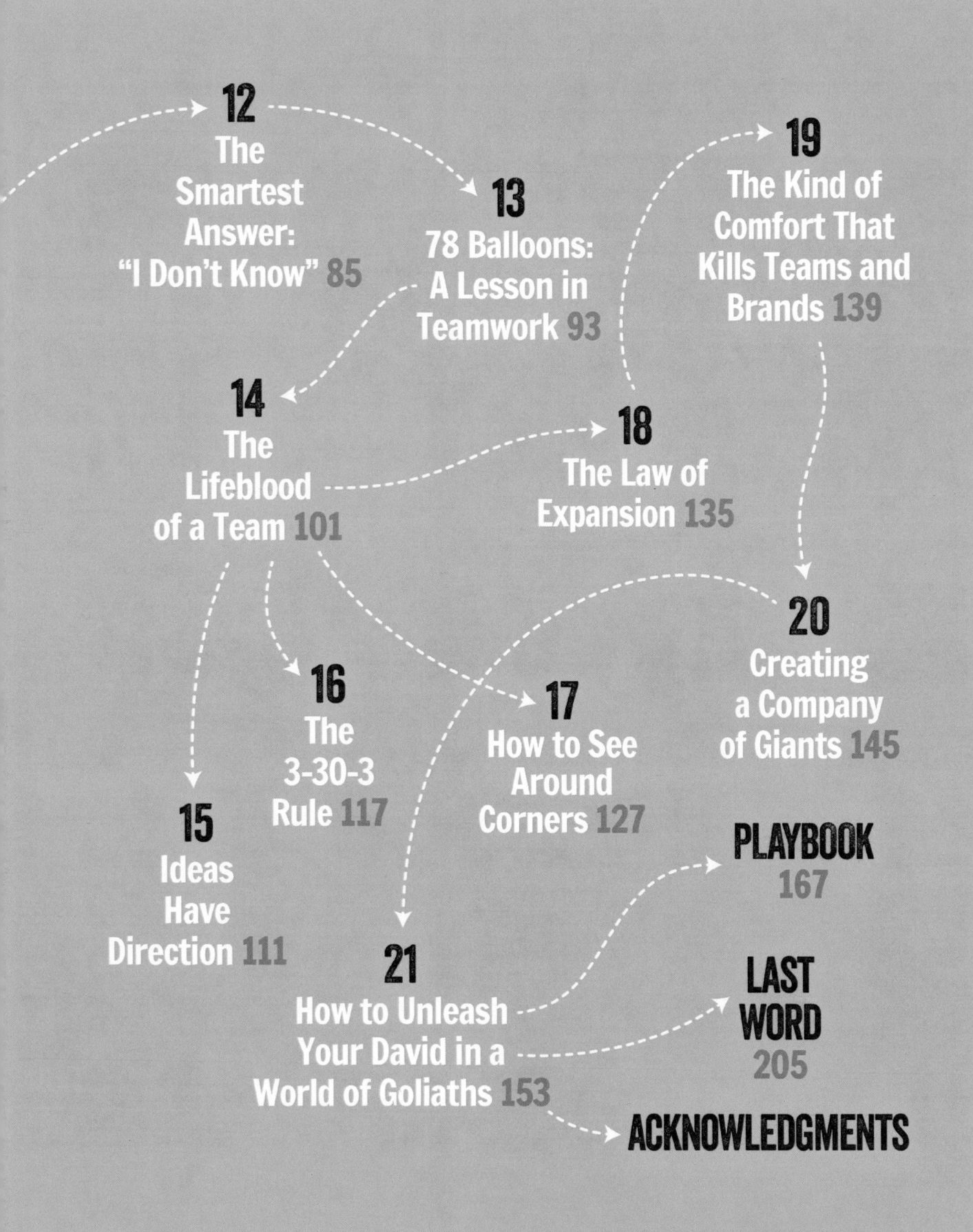

ACKNOWLEDGMENTS

"To surrender dreams — this may be madness. Too much sanity may be madness and maddest of all: to see life as it is, and not as it should be."

Cervantes
from Don Quixote
the first modern novel

Foreword
CLAUDE SILVER

Whether you're talking about brands or cultures, people matter. Both inside the organization and outside the organization.

Inside, it defines the culture. Outside, it defines the customer or client experience.

During the course of my career, I have worked on both the agency side and client side, which has given me a unique perspective on what winning teams have in common.

That path led to me being the world's first Chief Heart Officer, a position created for me by Gary Vaynerchuk. This has given me the perfect "home" at VaynerX to empower the 2,000+ hearts and minds that I serve.

Which is why I was so excited when David asked me to write the Foreword to **Rich Brand Poor Brand** because of a vision we both share: the role of people in creating brands and inspiring movements that inspire more people and fuel dreams.

David Brier once said to me, in reference to the friendship he and I share, "when we interchange, it's kind of like we are two jazzers who have hung out together for a while. The ones who get on stage, and there's just a synergy. It flows... that's what it feels like when we talk."

Being a layperson when it comes to jazz, the way I would return that sentiment to David is this, "Our friendship has so much spirit. We never deplete the well; rather we empower each other to rise up and get busy!"

THE BLANK CANVAS

I am often asked what my favorite question is to ask in an interview with a potential candidate. Funny enough, it's this: "If you had a blank canvas in front of you, draw a picture of your perfect job. Not the job you are applying for, but your idea of the perfect role."

Why you might ask is this my favorite? Because it allows the candidate to dream big.

It allows that person to color outside of any perceived lines, and in doing so, it offers me the ability to see if they are creating a job for themselves or what they think I want to see.

I am not looking for a recreated job description. I am looking for creativity. I am looking for joy and inspiration. I am looking for teamwork and leadership. I am looking to see what lights them up!

To me, this blank canvas symbolizes what is possible. Not what has potential but actually what can be created together with self-awareness, grit, and action. And let's admit it, in this moment, anything is possible.

So why now?

Because the gift of a blank canvas is that it is free of rules, free of emotion, and free of history.

After discussing this book with David, I saw that it represents a blank canvas of people, of discovery, of collaboration. It's the ultimate blank canvas of "What if?"

Rich Brand Poor Brand leaves you free to explore. And discover. And challenge what's come before... and to introduce something new.

PEOPLE ARE AT THE HEART OF IT ALL

Why am I talking about "people stuff" in a book called **Rich Brand Poor Brand?**

The answer is very simple. And very important.

At its core, brands only exist because of people. People who create brands. And people who are served by brands and share the values of those brands.

When David first explained this new book to me, he explained while **Brand Intervention** had all the tools to create a successful brand, some companies were still overlooking the vital role people played in the survival and success of their brands, starting with themselves and flowing outward to those they served as employees and customers.

Our greatest gift is the ability to give.

If we are not serving the world, then we are merely taking up space.

The day has come for all of us (and this includes those of us who are entrusted with brands) to move from a sense of entitlement and separation to a sense of belonging.

Remembering that there is always enough to go around is what is going to get you from good to great and from great to exceptional.

Building a bridge to bring us together on this journey is what David's metaphor of the two of us "being jazzers" is all about.

Rich Brand Poor Brand wakes us up to the possibilities of what we can all create together, walking across that bridge toward progress.

That is what this book is all about.

It's our legacy. Let's light it up.

Claude Silver
Chief Heart Officer
VaynerX

Claude Silver and me at VaynerX offices, Hudson Yards, NYC.

"It's alright to be Goliath but always act like David."

Phil Knight
NIKE

Introduction

How do you determine if you're a rich brand or a poor one?

By knowing what to measure.

Measuring the wrong thing (or things) can mistakenly "seem great" at first but result in things remaining unchanged (or contracting).

But by measuring the right factors, you expand your influence, your impact, and your relevance.

Being a **richer brand** isn't measured by the size of your company, the number of employees, or the amount of revenue that's produced.

There are some very large companies with very crappy brands and some much smaller companies with incredible, richer brands.

How?

Because **richer brands** are richer by a different set of metrics.

It's in how they solve problems for their clients:

They are richer than the obstacles they seek to overcome.

They are richer in approach than those who came before them.

They are richer in ingenuity than a large, cumbersome company with lots of bureaucratic red tape, internal politics, and a lack of team autonomy and nimbleness.

They are richer because they're selling the right thing and don't confuse what they make or deliver with what the customer is actually buying.

Because they are richer, they are more limber and able to react more swiftly.

DOES SIZE MATTER?

Ever experience something or someone "being bigger" than you?

Here's what happened: at that moment, you shrank back into yourself and felt that something (or someone) was bigger than you. You "got smaller."

At that precise point, that thing became "the bigger player" independent of facts or resources. To that extent, it had the apparency of being "richer" than us on some level.

How is this possible?

Because before facts and resources, a decision was made.

Claude Silver calls it, "the importance of taking up space."

BIG IDEAS REQUIRE SPACE

The bottom line: brands are about ideas and people.

Not only the people we serve but the people we work and play with. Those with whom we align our efforts.

Every day, people in business make decisions that make them richer **or** poorer, making their teams invigorated **or** depleted and making their customers loyal zealots **or** transient "flings" at the cash register.

This book is about the decisions that make us richer, make our teams more influential, make our customers loyal ambassadors for our creations, and make our allies and partners as wealthy as we are.

This is why **Rich Brand Poor Brand** has to do with brands and the role of the people who create them, making each richer, no matter the industry, no matter the location, and no matter their resources.

Here's to being an inspiration to many and the envy of those who insist on remaining smaller.

David Brier

"Without a team, your life won't be measured in years or even months."

"It will be measured in hours."

Luther (Ving Rhames) and Benji telling Grace in Mission Impossible: Dead Reckoning, Part I

1

The secret sauce for sustainable growth

Too many companies are playing the wrong game.

Instead of "How do we sell more?" They need to ask this:

- → "How do we help more?"

- → "How do we empower others more?"

- → "How do we make others more independent?"

Don't believe it? Try this:

The next time you feel stuck, ask:

→ **"How do I help another solve this?"**

The next time you feel confused, ask:

→ **"How do I help another get clarity on this?"**

The next time you feel challenged, ask:

→ "How would I help another overcome this?"

THAT is the secret sauce.

Because it makes you BIGGER. Rather than shrinking into your own challenges.

The answer to any of these questions:

Always go bigger and do it with the end game of the group you're doing it with ending up more stable, stronger, and more aligned.

It's exactly what enabled David to defeat Goliath.

THE RICH BRAND is focused on solving the problems of others, widening your scope, your sphere of influence, and the progress of those we serve and work with. Anchoring your growth and progress to the growth and progress you help others achieve will yield the best progress in the greatest number.

THE POOR BRAND is only focused on solving the problems of itself and is intent only on its own progress. This also masks a shortsighted metric: If I focus on my growth and overlook the growth of those around me (i.e., team members, clients, customers, and those I mentor), have I really grown?

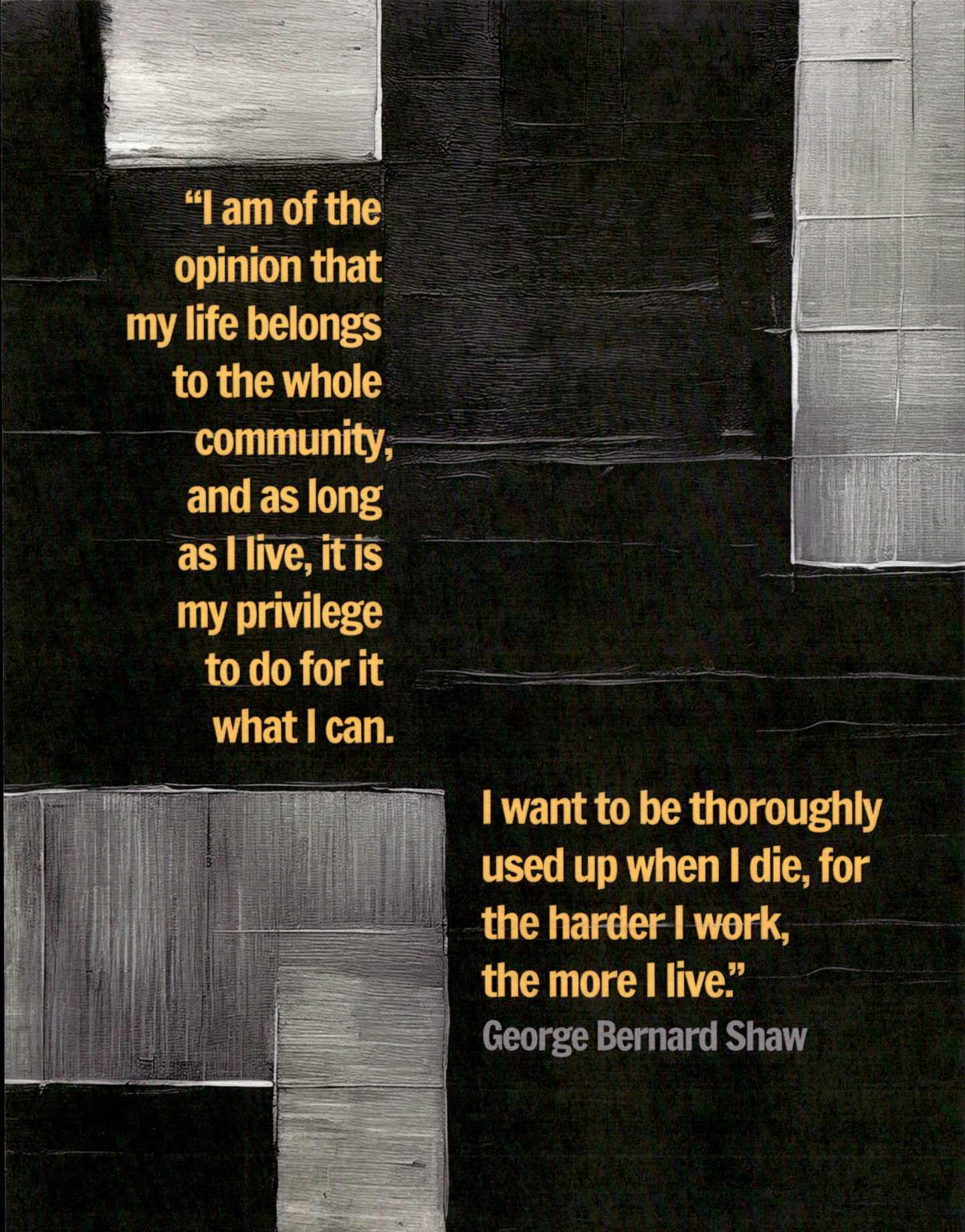

"I am of the opinion that my life belongs to the whole community, and as long as I live, it is my privilege to do for it what I can.

I want to be thoroughly used up when I die, for the harder I work, the more I live."

George Bernard Shaw

2

Fanatical intention

This concept came up during a discussion with multi-millionaire entrepreneur, Jeff Lerner, who empowers entrepreneurs worldwide.

In business and in life, we live in direct ratio to an invisible ingredient: the degree of fanatical intention we display to live a bigger role and how it is displayed in our actions with others: clients, customers,

colleagues, vendors,
and, of course, family.

This is because leadership
doesn't happen alone
in a bubble.

To survive fully,
we must connect.

To connect, we need to
recognize the necessity
of community.

With community, it all begins.

Those who seek to separate us into "this" or "that" tear us apart, making us doubtful of one another—only looking out for ourselves—forfeiting our power as a unified and aligned group.

THE RICH BRAND

sees power in the abilities of others and uses fanatical intention to unite them.

THE POOR BRAND

sees the opposite: strength achieved only through division, exhibiting fanatical intention only when groups are divided into self-centered group members. The only thing worse? Inviting someone to a party and insisting everyone sit in different rooms.

"Your work is going to fill a large part of your life, and the only way to be truly satisfied is to do what you believe is great work.

"And the only way to do great work is to love what you do."

Steve Jobs

3

The power of love

Want a great brand?

Fall in love. It works like this:

Great brands compel us.
They read our minds.
They reflect what's in our hearts. They "get us."

They inspire us to do things spontaneously.

They help us overcome indecision and stagnancy.

Without a second thought.

With a renewed sense
of what's possible.

Sounds almost like
love, doesn't it?

Yes. Yes, it does.

And like love, it takes
more than one to tango.

THE RICH BRAND knows that love is the ultimate commerce, especially since we make decisions with emotion and justify them with logic. Love is also special in this way: it's intoxicating, and the only commerce that truly compounds in all business growth.

THE POOR BRAND looks at transactions exclusively. The Poor Brand only looks at a spreadsheet (whereas The Rich Brand looks at the heartbeat), and fails to realize that monetary gain is a symptom of the only true building block of all business growth: love.

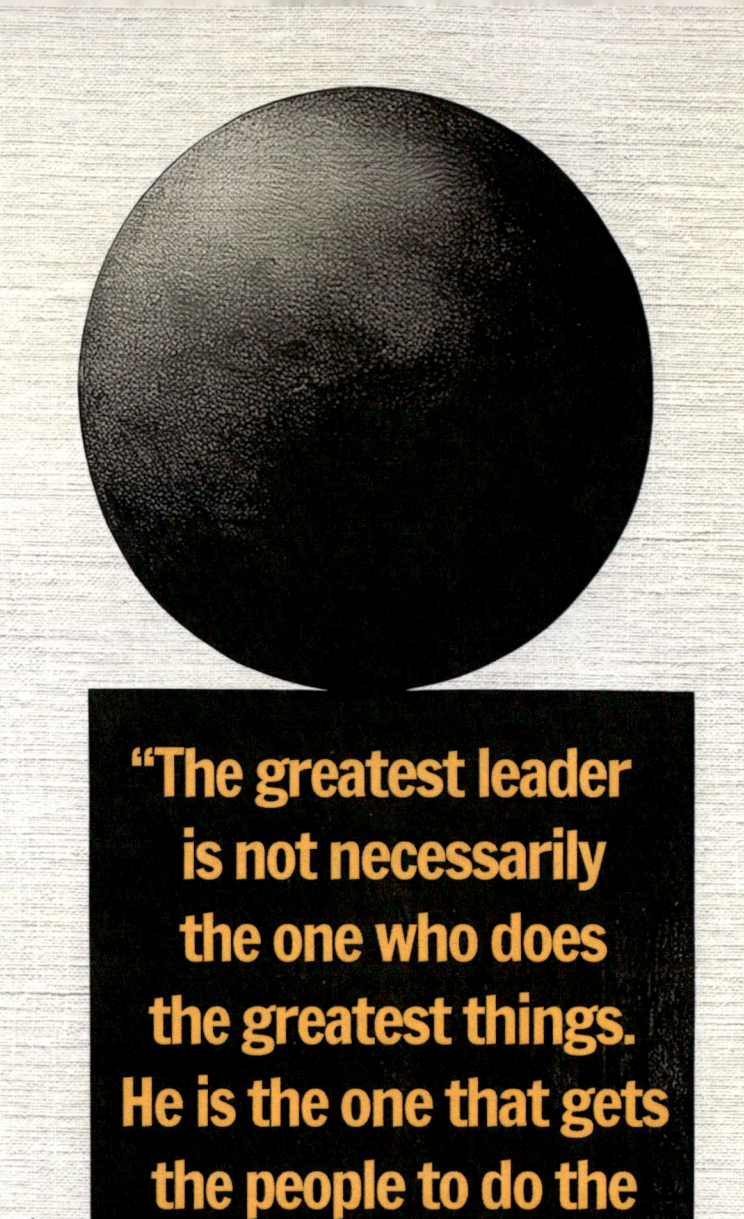

"The greatest leader is not necessarily the one who does the greatest things. He is the one that gets the people to do the greatest things."

Ronald Reagan
40th President of the United States

4

Others are the solution, not the problem

Every great leader embraces this.

It's how they create space: by growing **with** others rather than getting others out of the way.

It's why I say this about my wife, "I would sooner die with you rather than live without you."

In order to win, we must first take inventory.

We have to be able to honestly observe how others view the world and how they treat others. Having observed that, we use that trait as a metric, and we will never be blindsided again unless we excuse and explain away consistent offenses.

This is how Larry David and Jerry Seinfeld tapped into each other's comedic genius and used it to fuel the talents of Julia Louis-Dreyfus (Elaine), Jason Alexander (George), and Michael Richards (Kramer).

It's how Spielberg, Scorcese, Lucas, and Coppola formed a close-knit group in the 1970s and 1980s, frequently collaborating, sharing ideas, and supporting each other's projects.

It's how seven "misfits" from different colonies, backgrounds, and professions came together with a shared vision of breaking free from British rule, establishing a new nation, and writing the Declaration of Independence.

Each risked their lives, fortunes, and reputations in

the pursuit of a revolutionary idea: that a colony could overthrow its parent nation and establish a republic where the people had a voice in governance.

It's also how a small record label in Detroit, Michigan became a musical powerhouse that transformed the sound of American pop music.

Motown, unlike many other record labels, fostered a sense of family and community among its artists.

Artists, songwriters, and producers frequently collaborated, providing feedback and even competing in friendly challenges to outdo each other, all in the spirit of producing the next big hit.

The result? Motown had an astounding 79 records reaching the top ten of the Billboard Hot 100 between 1960 and 1969.

THE RICH BRAND

sees people as an irreplaceable asset embracing distinct talents and <u>not</u> confusing the excusing of someone else's bullshit with some variety of empathy. Confusing these two weakens the foundation of any empire and any brand.

THE POOR BRAND

tries to get things done "in spite of" other people and considers dealing with others something to overcome rather than something to channel for mutual expansion. The poor brand lacks the genius to turn "noise" into music.

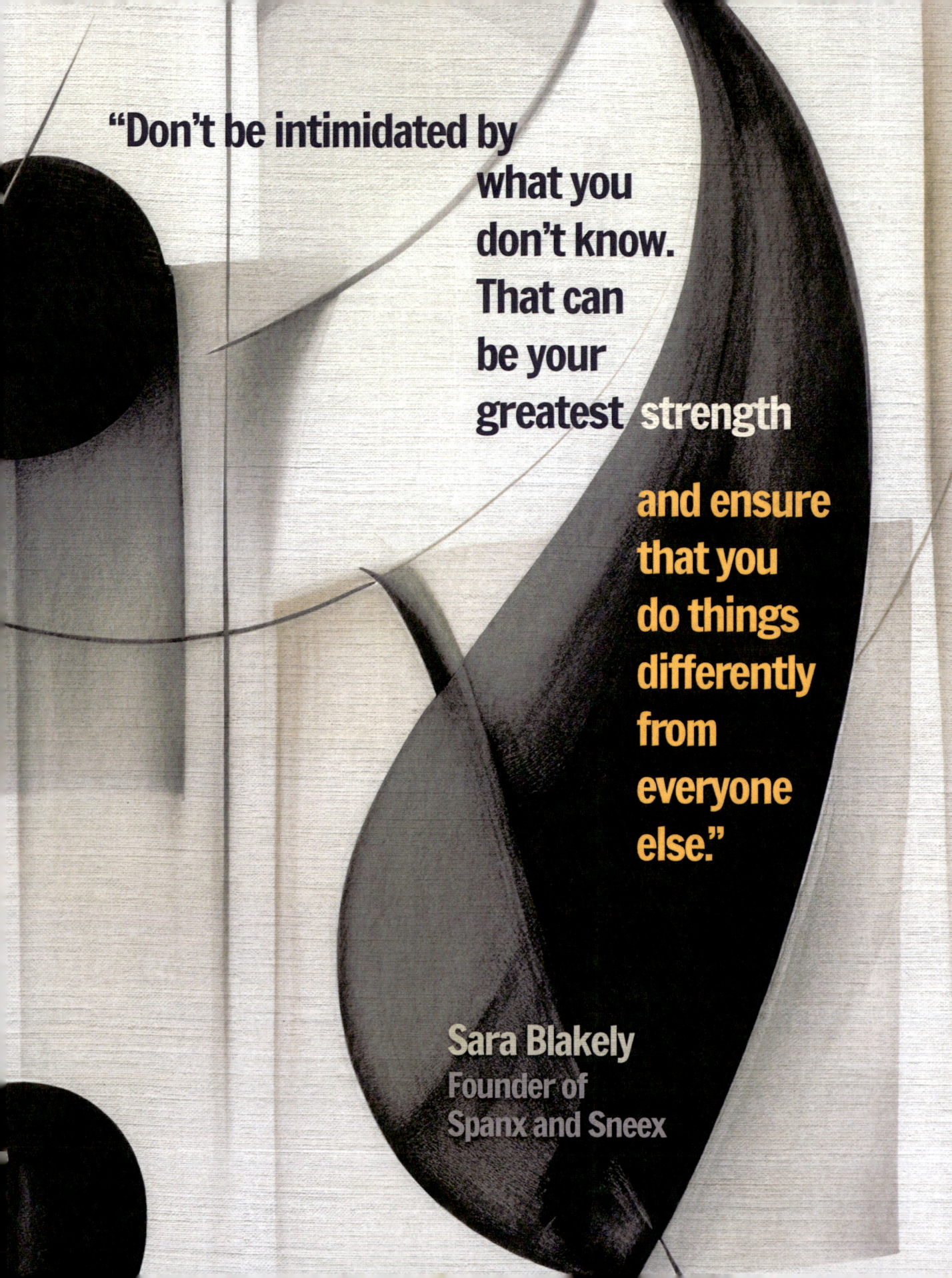

"Don't be intimidated by what you don't know. That can be your greatest strength and ensure that you do things differently from everyone else."

Sara Blakely
Founder of Spanx and Sneex

5

Not all differences are the same

I never thought I'd have to write this or say it, but here it is.

After the publication of **Brand Intervention**, some thought that in order to make their mark in the world, they simply had to "be different."

Unfortunately, I've witnessed too many entrepreneurs (who in attempting to do something meaningful and relevant) fail to discern between trivial differences (useless and microscopic ones) versus the kind of differences that are truly remarkable.

Remarkable? Yes.

The fact is, to make a difference in business and life in our dealings with others, we need to rise up to the standard of offering and providing something remarkable in what we provide to others. That means "something worth remarking about."

Predictable, average, and formulaic solutions do not meet that standard and let everyone down.

What's this got to do with branding? Everything, since so much is being automated and made impersonal. Hello A.I.

In today's world, it's our job to turn the ordinary into the extraordinary, from a greeting in person or on the phone, to the packaging materials we put our products in, to the way our words, images, and messages are presented to the world.

Anything less is insufficient to have any lasting impact in today's noisy world.

THE RICH BRAND recognizes that people take note of differences, attention to detail, and attention to the thousand "little things" that say "you matter." The Rich Brand appreciates the opportunity to make every moment a standout moment that celebrates the true power differences make in the lives of others.

THE POOR BRAND

lacks the ability to see the compounding effect differences bring about and only looks at transactions and immediate returns and then wonders why customers strayed elsewhere.

Elaine:
"It shrinks?"

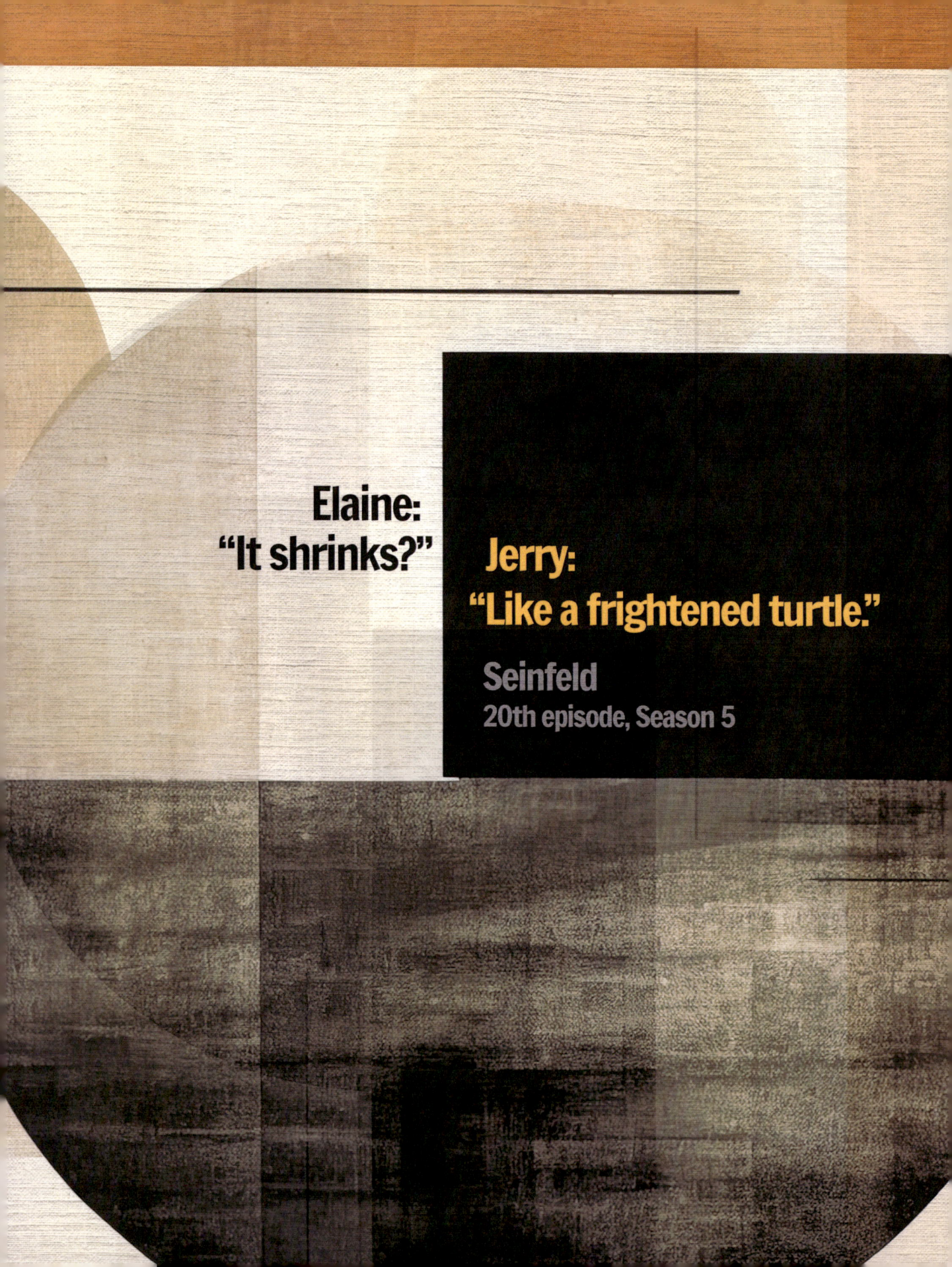

Jerry:
"Like a frightened turtle."

Seinfeld
20th episode, Season 5

6

Is shrinkage your enemy?

A brand does NOT **restrain** you and put you or your brand in a box. In fact, it does the opposite. The right answer liberates you and pushes you toward being the richer brand.

If what you're doing is not liberating you, it's **not** right.

If it scares you a bit, that's a good thing. You're expanding into new terrain, and that always means new, unfamiliar ground.

With unfamiliarity, you will make some mistakes, and work through some misestimations to nail what works. These mistakes are lessons in what doesn't work.

The rule is: keep at it because stopping is the only way to fail.

Continue to get back up saying "no" to two things: failure and shrinking.

Shrinkage is choosing comfort and familiarity instead of courage and initiative.

Always embrace unfamiliarity that accompanies growth instead of "familiar comfort" that invariably results in shrinkage of one sort or another.

THE RICH BRAND

is confident that continuous expansion in one's skills, connections, and community is the only reliable road to lasting prosperity and growth.

THE POOR BRAND

is comfortable traveling along the beaten path. Something to remember: there's a reason it's called beaten. ;-)

"The most courageous act is still to think for yourself. Aloud."

Coco Chanel

7

The "taking small steps" myth

The most painful experience I have is when speaking with a team member, founder, CEO, client or vendor who says this:

"Interesting. OK, we'll try 20% of what you recommend and see if it works."

It won't, and here's why.

We all know the 80/20 rule:

- 20% of clients represents 80% of your revenue.

- **Same is true for advertising: 20% of it gets you 80% of your sales.**

- **Same for social media, outbound efforts, personnel, etc.**

So, if 20% of anything gets you 80% of your results, let's look at the above math:

20% is a little dip into what might work. So when we

refuse to test it out fully (even in a smaller test market), that "20% effort" equates to about 4%.

That is why this approach of "let's do a little and see if it works" doesn't work out.

Four percent of anything achieves nothing in life, in career, in branding.

It's why multi-tasking is so unproductive and is now frowned upon by efficiency and production experts.
A lot of busy-ness on too many things and too little focus on any one thing.

It's simply too little. (This takes us back to the mandate to not shrink and be small).

Ask any leader, or any great salesperson, or any influencer. They'll tell you.

THE RICH BRAND isn't scared to lean in. Instead, The Rich Brand leans in fully, refuses to take small, tentative steps, and doesn't expect a bigger result than the effort that was put in.

THE POOR BRAND does not take the steps necessary to discover what makes us happy to work there, shop there, or enjoy a little time there. Instead, small, tentative steps are taken, leaving out the courage needed to win (or fail and learn).

"Your attitude changes when your knowledge changes.

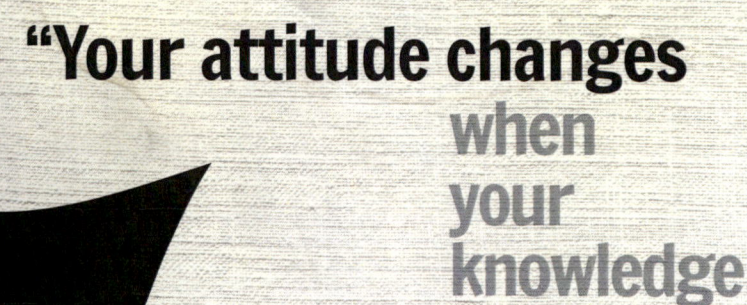

Your knowledge changes when your experiences change."

Kevin Hart

8

Reciprocation. The super glue that bonds

There is one key metric that too few entrepreneurs and CEOs know and use proactively.

Before I spell it out, let's look at what we respond to.

How does it feel when someone holds the door for you?

Or makes room for you on a bus or train?

Or says hello in a store?

Or calls you (not emails you) after the sale to ensure you were happy?

Each of those is a form of reciprocation: a general kindness and graciousness toward others.

It's increasingly rare these days in life in general and even less in business.

And while reciprocation is defined as "responding to (a gesture or action) by making a corresponding one," this is commonly seen as a response to something that happened earlier.

But there's a more subtle use.

Instead of someone doing a very obvious gesture and us responding to that, there is simply "reciprocating" another's presence, granting it recognition.

So when someone shows up in your store, that is a gesture of trust. We can reciprocate in kind.

Or when someone takes a moment to look at us, or text us, and validate something we've shared or posted online.

Each is a gesture that we can reciprocate with a comparable gesture.

And there's another layer that is actually how I've become friends with some of the most respected and influential thought leaders in the world.

It started with me simply expressing my appreciation for something they did.

I had no ulterior motive. I simply wanted to thank them for doing what they did, said, or wrote.

I noticed a pattern: the nicest of them reciprocated with a comment, note, or message of some sort. The others never replied at all.

And those who reciprocated quickly became friends and were open to connecting.

And this taught me a new metric: How quickly does another reciprocate?

If their response is slow or nonexistent, that's worth noting. Move on.

If their response is fast and on-point, note that as well.

Why?

Because how quickly or slowly they reciprocate displays:

→ the speed of their observation.

→ the speed of their ability to extrapolate.

→ their recognition of others and their role in survival.

→ the speed of their going into action.

And the people who you'll be able to create amazing things with will also be the ones who naturally reciprocate. Use this metric and win.

THE RICH BRAND

demonstrates a speed of recognition. A recognition of others. The Rich Brand gives freely, reciprocates quickly, and grants importance to others.

THE POOR BRAND

is the slow brand. Slow to recognize. Slow to adapt. Slow to self-correct. Worst of all, The Poor Brand is slow to respond or reciprocate and doesn't grant importance to others.

"From everyone who has been given much, much will be demanded; and from the one who has been entrusted with much, much more will be asked."

Daymond John
Founder of FUBU and Shark Tank star

9

The power skill they don't teach you in school

IQ and EQ are passé.

We hear about EQ (Emotional Quotient) as being a vital component.

The more powerful metric we must speak about is AQ (Admiration Quotient): the degree to which we admire. It's how we value, elevate, and empower anyone we work with including colleagues, protégés, and employees.

An amazing culture of people who have AQ in abundance will naturally trust one another, empower one another, and elevate one another in a contagious frenzy of awesomeness that others want to be part of.

THE RICH BRAND elevates others using admiration. The kind of admiration that gets others saying, "Oh look at you! Spreading admiration like confetti—so generous." It's like being nice for free and still somehow winning. ;-)

THE POOR BRAND

depends on the admiration of others and relies on that admiration to survive. It's like living life as though it were an Instagram post looking for more likes to feel it's worthy.

"A mind is like a parachute.
It doesn't work if it is not open."

Frank Zappa

10

True expertise vs. bullshit

True experts leave us feeling empowered. Capable. Independent.

THE RICH BRAND gives.

False experts leave us feeling reliant, certain of **their** genius, and dependent.

Dependence is bullshit.

THE POOR BRAND takes.

"The best revenge is massive success."

Frank Sinatra

11

"I don't care WTF the piano sounds like"

This is the story of a legendary jazz performance that almost didn't happen.

Its recording would become the best-selling solo jazz album in the world: The Köln Concert by Keith Jarrett.

The night was January 25, 1975. It happened after a sleepless 400-mile overnight car ride with his producer from the prior day's performance in Epalinges, Switzerland.

Jarrett, a prolific pianist, was known for his exacting precision without compromise.

For this performance, a night of piano improvisation, he'd requested an Imperial Bösendorfer piano, a near-ten-foot, eight-octave grand piano.

Having not slept during the car ride, Keith arrived exhausted. His back was in pain. And it didn't stop there.

The food they'd ordered for dinner took so long to arrive, Keith ended up having no time to eat his meal. And to top it off, the concert hall was sold out.

On top of arriving hungry, being in pain and totally

exhausted, something else happened: the piano that was there was a poor impersonation of the piano he'd specified. Not only was it out of tune, it had several keys that wouldn't play and pedals that didn't work.

Keith and his producer were ready to tell the recording engineers to pack it up, tell the hall the concert was cancelled, and chalk it up to experience.

In spite of all these obstacles: no sleep, no food, no piano matching his specs, and having to now wear a back brace, Keith made a last-minute decision:

"I was forced to play in what was—at the time—a new way. Somehow I felt I had to bring out whatever qualities this instrument had... my sense was, 'I have to do this. I'm doing it. I don't care what the f**k the piano sounds like.'"

The result? Legacy. A true celebration of an artist, his instrument, his audience, and the room to improvise and discover with no safety net.

THE RICH BRAND

adapts and is ready to shift gears. Quickly. Without excuses. And without a safety net of "reasons why we can't" welcoming the moment we joyously ask, "Where the hell are we?"

THE POOR BRAND is accustomed to running on empty, unable to shift gears, is quick to blame, slow to adapt, and prone to switching lanes before a pothole is ever actually seen.

Rey asked,
"Is that even possible?"

"I never ask that question
until after I've done it."
Han Solo
"Star Wars:
The Force Awakens"

12

The smartest answer: "I don't know"

The smartest and most productive groups (and entrepreneurs) I've ever known have several traits in common:

1. They are always curious.

2. The intelligence of others doesn't intimidate them, it excites them.

3. Acknowledging that they don't know doesn't scare them.

4. New ideas strengthen their resolve to discover more and question more.

5. Admitting "I don't know" is an asset not a liability.

The worst accounts and most unhappy entrepreneurs were the ones who approached the project with the attitude, "I have nothing new to learn here."

When a person can no longer dream, they've dried up.

When an artist can no longer be inspired by something new, their career is over.

When a company feels "we have it all figured out" is the day another company comes along with a new innovation and invents a new category.

At the foundation of every breakthrough is an "I don't know" moment.

Being able to say, "I don't know," and questioning things is the first step to new plateaus for a group, its team, and its work.

Want to break through? Create a culture that embraces the "I don't know" moments.

THE RICH BRAND is nourished by curiosity and not threatened by not knowing. Every spark of genius starts with asking questions like a toddler on caffeine but somehow ending up with a fortune instead of sticky fingers. Turns out, "I don't know" is basically code for "I'm about to own this."

THE POOR BRAND is threatened by questioning anything and being vulnerable enough to say, "I don't know" and overlooking this one fact: It's hard to say "I don't know" when you're busy pretending you do.

"Service to others is the rent you pay for your room here on Earth."

Muhammad Ali

13

78 Balloons: A lesson in teamwork

I came across a compelling story online. It was impossible to find who originated it.

But it perfectly illustrates a crucial point for team building and branding which is why you're reading this now. It goes like this:

A university professor had each student write their name on a balloon.

They were collected and put in a large mesh net.

The mesh net then opened, and the balloons fell upon the sea of students.

The challenge:

"Find the balloon with your name amongst the bunch falling from the ceiling. You have five minutes."

Success meant finding their own balloon; failure meant not.

Although each tried to find the ballon with their name on it, no one succeeded. Not a single student.

Despite their best efforts, 100% failure.

The professor put the balloons back and had new

instructions, "Catch a balloon and give it to its owner."

Same action. Completely different context.

The task was completed in under three minutes.

He concluded, "Happiness is like these balloons. If we only seek our own, we won't find it. But when we help others find theirs, we find ours too."

Want to kick Goliath's ass? Help another find their balloon.

As true for team members as it is for clients.

THE RICH BRAND looks out for others first, like finding a lost dog and helping it find its rightful owner—everyone's happy, tails are wagging, and love is in the air. All of a sudden, fetching success doesn't seem so out of reach.

THE POOR BRAND

overlooks this factor: winning means nothing without others to play with and play for. Without anyone else to play with, they just end up being that person in the park throwing a ball...to no one.

"Content is not just for monetization. Content is really for relationships."

Jason Feifer
Entrepreneur Magazine
Editor in Chief

14

The lifeblood of a team

The truly successful pay attention to two vital components of human interaction. Each involves the lifeblood of a team:

1. The first factor tackles what weakens a team. The answer is pretty simple: by reducing that group to individual entities and separating these entities from one another.

To be clear, I am not talking about what makes you uniquely you. That is something priceless and irreplaceable.

In contrast, I am talking about something quite different, something that detaches us from our real connection to our team members.

When what we do is at the expense of others—that is the line that divides and weakens us.

This is the way others distract, divide, and defeat any group:

By making each team member an individual, this "individual" becomes a separate piece. This makes each team member doubtful of their fellow team members, doubtful of themselves, and, worst of all, only looking out for themselves.

As a result, each team member forfeits their power as a unified and aligned group member.

2. The second factor addresses what strengthens a team. This comes down to each team member knowing one fact:

being bigger (and richer as a brand) is an idea and an assumed role.

A community that operates this way realizes its own survival is only enhanced as others thrive and grow.

It's the idea that there's plenty to go around.

It has enough confidence to stay focused on the bigger goal and doesn't erode away and quibble over small hiccups.

In fact, this second factor rejects the inclination to shrink down into small turf wars and instead looks at how to make more win as part of the optimal outcome.

THE RICH BRAND knows success is a buffet, not a packed lunch. Like that one person at a party who brings snacks for everyone—because they know if the whole group's happy and winning, there's more cake to go around.

THE POOR BRAND is really out to lunch. Like someone guarding their hors d'oeuvres at a feast. They think protecting that one soggy triangle is all that matters. Why settle for crumbs when you can feast on the whole buffet?

"In a way, we are magicians.

We are alchemists, sorcerers and wizards.

We are a very strange bunch.

But there is great fun in being a wizard."

Billy Joel

15

Ideas have direction

There's one thing we all do: we each have ideas.

Some ideas go inward. Some go in all directions. Others go outward.

Ideas going outward, benefitting the most people, are the things worth feeding.

Pay attention to the direction others offer you in the way of ideas.

Some ideas are built on growth.

Some are built on destruction—relying on the failure of others to win.

Others are built on conservation (which is built on the idea that creation is a scarce commodity). That is false and destructive. Trust me.

No matter what, remember: ideas have direction.

THE RICH BRAND knows the true power that results from the quality of ideas and **how much** they are shared outwardly. Like handing out sunshine on a cloudy day—the more we extend outward, the more everyone feels the warmth.

THE POOR BRAND

has long forgotten the power of an idea, replacing rays of sunshine with cynicism (which I call "the energy drink of doom"). It only looks at what's coming inward and has lost sight of the importance to give outwardly.

"Learn the rules like a pro, so you can break them like an artist."

Pablo Picasso

16

The 3-30-3 Rule

I hate rules and templates (except this one).

It's the 3-30-3 Rule: Winning the War for Attention.

I love this rule. I use it all the time, and it works like this.

Today, we have:

→ **3 seconds to get attention (stop the scroll)**

→ **30 seconds to validate their curiosity**

→ **3 minutes to leave your mark**

Here's how it works in real time:

3 SECONDS TO CAPTURE ATTENTION

In **Brand Intervention**, I talked about the shortness of attention spans:

8 seconds before a person flicks onto something else.

This is talking about the amount of time to hook your audience.

Picture this: Your audience's attention is like a Shark Tank investor.

In just 3 seconds, you need to hook them.

How? Craft a headline (or ice breaker) that's as irresistible as a billion-dollar pitch and as convincing as the next big unicorn.

This is your first bold move.

30 SECONDS TO IGNITE CURIOSITY

Got their attention? Good.

Now, you have 30 seconds to pass the sniff test.

Dazzle with new, compelling facts, not regurgitations of stuff we've all heard before.

Blow their minds with fresh insights.

Weave a narrative as gripping as a John Grisham novel.

Make every second count.

Why does this work?

Because people don't come to new conclusions with old information.

3 MINUTES TO REWARD THEM
You've got them on the hook. Now reel them in.

In 3 minutes, your message must resonate deeply.

Don't just "fill the time" — fill their minds with gold.

Have them say, "I am so glad you showed up today. I needed this."

And here's the craziest part:

This works just as well in meetings, sales, and pitches as it does for social media and content.

THE RICH BRAND

embraces how fractured attention is these days and rewards others for their investment of time and attention.

THE POOR BRAND

ignores the high value of time, and plows ahead ignoring the "warning signs" of indifference.

"There is no greater mistake than to try to leap into an abyss in two jumps."

David Lloyd George
former UK Prime Minister

17

How to see around corners

James Clear talks about the power of small changes and the building blocks of new habits in his book, *Atomic Habits*.

Develop those and they will compound and change your life.

Here's how to elevate this into a genius level:

Pay attention to and notice "micro-shifts" in life, in people, in industries, and in culture.

Unfortunately, many of us are too busy to notice these.

But those amongst us who can see those changes and shifts will "see things before they happen."

These people we consider geniuses—they detected something before it was noticed en masse.

The richest brands do this, taking note of and observing "micro-shifts."

The greatest investors do this. The finest athletes do this.

They pay attention to subtle shifts that change what we

talk about, what we value, what we choose to purchase. They see patterns developing before they become big sweeping changes.

The poorest brands are only focused on what's happening now, the current deal, this week's quota. They never see what's coming. Until it's too late.

THE RICH BRAND spots micro-shifts like a detective catching the villain in the first act—seeing the little bits of "evidence" before they become tsunamis of proof, long before anyone else has gotten the scent or read the memo.

THE POOR BRAND

is too busy staring at its own shoes to notice the changes (those micro-shifts) right under its nose or what's right around the corner.

"Success doesn't come from what you do occassionally, it comes from what you do consistently."

Marie Forleo

18

The law of expansion

If what you're doing isn't demanding you be ingenious, the game you're playing is not big enough. Don't underestimate how amazing you can be.

THE RICH BRAND embraces all challenges to flex its ingenuity.

The lesson: Keep widening your sphere of influence. Playing the bigger game will feel more alive. Heck, you may even break into a sweat. And that's a good thing.

THE POOR BRAND shrinks under the pressure to be ingenious.

"When we own our stories, we get to write a brave new ending."

Brené Brown

19

The kind of comfort that kills teams & brands

The bigger problem will challenge you.

It will test you, push you, and stretch you.

Most importantly, it will unite you.

Why? Because small problems divide us. Small problems keep everyone internalized and operating in an isolated way.

But bigger problems? They're the ones we must tackle together. They unite us because, with them, we have a common external enemy and a purpose toward outsmarting and overcoming this obstacle.

Small problems keep us separated and inward. Big problems get us expanding, focusing outward.

The biggest threat we each face is getting comfortable with "small games" and being too busy to remember the big ones we're capable of achieving.

THE RICH BRAND

stays focused on what's out there, knowing the more we do that, the greater our survival as a team is.

THE POOR BRAND thinks survival requires "protecting one's gains" and loses sight of the fact of how much territory was forfeited when making this choice.

"If each of us hires people who are smaller than we are, we shall become a company of dwarfs.

"But, if each of us hires people who are bigger than we are, we shall become a company of giants."

Warren Buffett

20

Creating a company of giants

Our ability to create is more powerful than any "cushion" because "cushions" become a crutch.

They become a "safety net" where we hold back or "get comfortable and complacent" because there's always a Plan B.

Leaders know this as stagnancy.

It's our weakest point
of vulnerability that our
competition will always
take advantage of.

Your greatest safety net?
Your ability to create.

Nothing can stop
that, or top that.

Sometimes the idea
you come up with is an
impossible one, one that

everybody has relegated to "inevitable failure."

As my friend Jasmin Alić wrote, "Most people don't fail. They quit."

What if instead of quitting, you simply chose to create more?

What you need to know is this:

The idea of "impossible" is always preceded by an innovation, a breakthrough, a "why-didn't-we-think-of-that?" insight that leaves others in admiration.

Or envious.

THE RICH BRAND knows there's power in creation and weakness in any "safety net." This means no Plan B. No cushion "just in case." Instead, it's pure guts and unbridled creativity. Why does this work? Because we're too busy tightrope-walking over anyone else's complacency.

THE POOR BRAND lacks the persistence and stamina necessary to create more, imagine more, and defy more, like someone sitting on the couch binge-watching the latest Netflix marathon explaining why they don't win athletic marathons. Instead, ditch the Cheetos and put on your Nikes.

"Learn to work harder on yourself than you do on your job.

If you work hard on your job, you can make a living, but if you work hard on yourself, you'll make a fortune."

Jim Rohn

21

How to unleash your David in a world of Goliaths

Goliaths are cumbersome and nowhere near as nimble as you.

That is your superpower.

Here's your **Rich Brand Poor Brand** checklist to put all of this into action:

1. **Empower Others →** Shift focus from sales and pitches to empowering colleagues and customers.

Help others grow, and your brand will thrive.

2. **Fanatical Intention** →
To survive fully, we must connect. To connect, we need to recognize the necessity of community. Own that.

3. **The Power of Love** →
Want a killer brand? Fall in love with your customers. When they

feel the love, they'll move mountains for you.

4. **Others Are the Solution** → See people as your secret weapon, not obstacles. Collaborate, celebrate, and create magic together.

5. **Not All Differences Are the Same** → Don't just be different—be remarkable. Offer something so unique

and powerful, people can't stop talking about you.

6. **Why Shrinkage Is Your Enemy** → Take risks, embrace the unknown, and expand like your life depends on it—because it does.

7. **The "Taking Small Steps" Myth** → Dip your toe in, and you'll drown. Go all-in on your ideas,

because half-assed efforts get you nowhere.

8. **Reciprocation** → Be the brand that gives generously and responds quickly. Watch how fast people flock to you.

9. **The Power Skill They Don't Teach You in School** → Admiration is your God-given superpower. Elevate others, and

you'll create an unstoppable force of positivity and growth.

10. **True Expertise vs. Bullshit** → Real experts lift us up; fake ones keep us down. Be the brand that empowers and watch your company and your clients soar.

11. **"I Don't Care WTF the Piano Sounds Like"** → When life throws you curveballs, hit them out of the park. No excuses—just adapt, thrive, and own the game.

12. **The Smartest Answer— "I Don't Know"** → Curiosity didn't kill the cat—it made it a freakin' genius. Admit when you don't know

and prepare for some serious breakthroughs.

13. **78 Balloons—A Lesson in Teamwork** → Help others find their balloon, and you'll find yours. Success was never a solo mission; it's always been a team sport.

14. **The Lifeblood of a Team** → Unity is your secret sauce. Keep your team tight

and focused on the big win. Every day. And you'll crush any obstacle.

15. **Ideas Have Direction** →
Feed ideas that take you higher and be obsessed to help others win. It's not about you—it's about the ripple effect you create.

16. **The 3-30-3 Rule** →
Hook them in 3 seconds, dazzle them in 30, and

leave them begging for more in 3 minutes. The relationship between time invested and value gotten has never been higher.

17. **How to See Around Corners** → Become a "tiny shift ninja." Spot the tiny shifts before anyone else does. The brands that see the future before it hits are the ones that win.

18. **The Law of Expansion** →
If it doesn't challenge you, it dilutes your resolve. Play bigger, dig deeper, go wider, and let your ingenuity run wild.

19. **The Kind of Comfort That Kills Teams and Brands** →
Small problems are organizational fast food— tasty but deadly. Chase the

big, hairy challenges that push you to greatness.

20. **Creating a Company of Giants** → Lean into the impossible, keep creating, and watch as your "crazy ideas" turn into world-changing innovations.

Ready to see this in action?

In the next chapter, I show you how others have done it.

"Those who do, DO."

"Those who don't, WON'T."

David Brier

RICH BRAND POOR BRAND
Playbook

You've made it to the Playbook. Well done. It's here that you'll see how others have used Rich Brand Poor Brand principles to grow their brands, unleash the power of their groups, and increase their impact. At right are some of the companies that have thrown out Poor Brand mindsets and habits and replaced them with Rich Brand actions and behavior. And on the following pages, I share with how I helped them and how you can use these for your team, collaborators, and customers. After that, you'll want to re-read **Rich Brand Poor Brand** from the beginning to boldly go where no David has gone before.

SELF RENEW

CELLULAR HEALTH. CELLULAR NUTRITION. CELLULAR VITALITY.

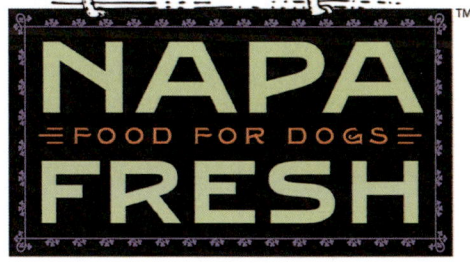

PARTNERS GRIT

BLACK SHEEP
ESTD 2011
CULINARY ARTS

smarthair SOCIETY

Lifelong ACCESS

KARLI CENTER

nimbl
FREEDOM TO ROAM

1st first search

NAPA FRESH
FOOD FOR DOGS
EARTH'S MOST CIVILIZED FOOD FOR DOGS

Let's Roll
MADE IN THE USA
PERFECT MOTORCYCLE STORAGE

store connect

xcitium
The Power of Zero. Unleashed.

The Power of Zero. Unleashed.

Bringing sports to life
True Winners

Here's how we helped High Meadow Farms rebrand: Instead of focusing on selling their raw dog food, we focused on the dog owners—their lifestyle, passions, and daily moments of joy.

That shift led to a new name: Napa Fresh Food for Dogs, capturing what matters to their audience—fresh air, rolling hills, family, and their furry companions. Sometimes, the biggest opportunity for growth is right in front of you.

Action tip: Isolate your customer's values and aspirations. Use that insight to help your customers "find their balloon."

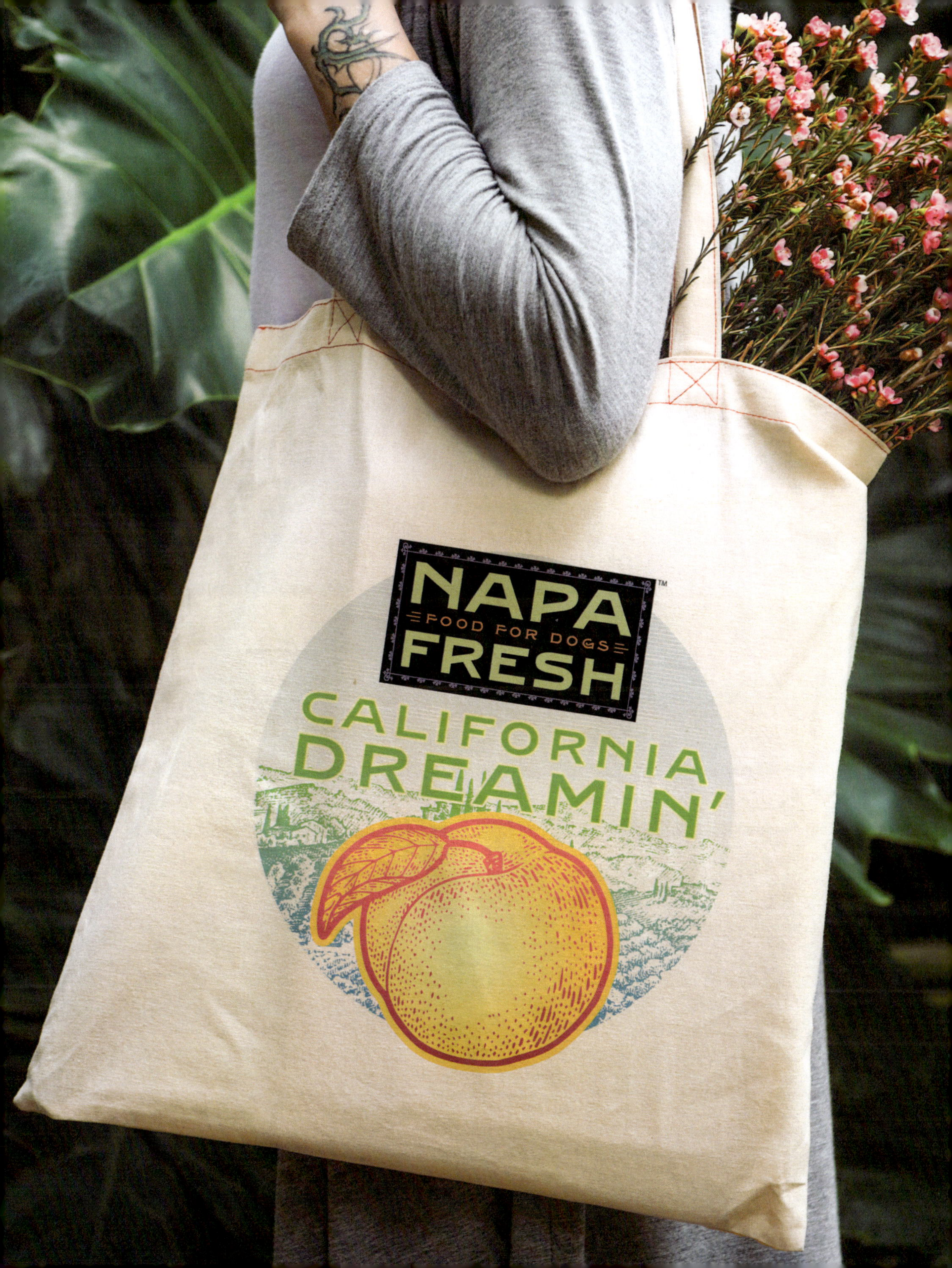
NAPA
FOOD FOR DOGS
FRESH
™
CALIFORNIA
DREAMIN'

NAPA FOOD FOR DOGS FRESH
BISCUITS
NAPA FRESH
CULINARY GRADE
INGREDIENTS
FROM THE USA
FOOD FOR DOGS
NAPA FOOD FOR DOGS FRESH
BISCUITS
NAPA FRESH
CULINARY GRADE
INGREDIENTS
FROM THE USA
FOOD FOR DOGS
NAPA FRESH
CULINARY GRADE
INGREDIENTS
FROM THE USA
FOOD FOR DOGS

100% PURE
CULINARY
GRADE
INGREDIENTS
NAPA
FOOD FOR DOGS
FRESH
HEALTH TO THE MAX

RICH BRAND POOR BRAND PLAYBOOK

Choosing your battle with fanatical intention: In 1955, a group of parents in Illinois did something unheard of: they founded an alliance to support children with Intellectual or Developmental Disabilities (IDD). This became Marcfirst, a nonprofit which served individuals from early childhood through adulthood. There was only one problem.

People in need could wait up to a decade to get the help they needed. Hence, the new name, Lifelong Access, with the new slogan: Services needed. Barriers removed.

Action tip: Don't just remove obstacles—obliterate them. Own the fight that really matters and reshape the narrative to cut through the noise.

Lifelong
ACCESS
Services needed. Barriers removed.

Lifelong
ACCESS

Services needed.
Barriers removed.

Services needed.
Barriers removed.

RICH BRAND POOR BRAND PLAYBOOK

Unleash the power of love: The rebrand of Belly Barbecue was a complete overhaul—keeping the award-winning recipes and tossing out everything else. The original label was branding anarchy: blending American, English, and Japanese influences into a confusing message.

We stripped it down, rebranded it as Black Sheep Culinary Arts, with the new product line Bloom™ Sauce & Marinade. The concept? Help home cooks unleash flavors and create "Instant Kitchen Redemption."

Action tip: Ensure those around you ditch what doesn't serve them—create a new category, own the story, and start spreading the love.

UNLEASH THE AMAZING FLAVOR OF YOUR
STEAK · POULTRY · SEAFOOD · VEGGIES
BLACK SHEEP
ESTD 2011
CULINARY ARTS
HANDCRAFTED · MADE IN SMALL BATCHES
BLOOM™
SAUCE AND MARINADE
INSTANT KITCHEN REDEMPTION™
ORIGINAL RECIPE
Net Wt 8 fl oz (236 mL)
GLUTEN-FREE RECIPE

RICH BRAND POOR BRAND PLAYBOOK

True expertise vs. bullshit: Mary's Toronto-based salon offered great hair coloring and treatments for curly-haired clients. But before rebranding it to Smart Hair Society, I had to pinpoint two things: 1) Who was competing for attention in this market? and 2) Was there a community of curly-haired people craving better solutions for their hair?

By identifying this, we built a brand based on knowledge (aka "smart") rewarding curiosity, thus creating a new category.

Action tip: Use your unique knowledge to authentically and selflessly empower those you serve and work with.

Say Hello to Your Get Out of Gel Card

smarthair SOCIETY

SHOW YOUR HAIR
THE INTELLIGENCE IT DESERVES

Understanding people, not algorithms, 5Xed this rebrand's growth: Motorcycle owners aren't some "algorithm"—they're people with passions. Yet so many brands skim over this point. Let's Roll, a manufacturer of top-tier motorcycle lifts and cruisers, saw 4.93X growth in 12 months after we rebranded them with that simple truth in mind.

Instead of treating customers as a demographic, we focused on what they really valued: convenience, smart space use, and respect for their prized possession.

Action tip: Tell everyone to stop chasing numbers. Treat the people you work with as real people and build something everyone cares about.

WE SHOW MOTORCYCLES
THE RESPECT THEY DESERVE

Let's Roll

MADE IN THE USA

PERFECT MOTORCYCLE STORAGE

CORE BRAND ELEMENTS

Let's Roll
MADE IN THE USA
PERFECT MOTORCYCLE STORAGE

Let's Roll
MADE IN THE USA

Let's Roll
MADE IN THE USA
CRUISER AND LIFT
PERFECT MOTORCYCLE STORAGE

PRODUCT PLAQUES

Let's Roll — MADE IN THE USA — **CRUISER**

Let's Roll — MADE IN THE USA — **LIFT**

MISCELLANEOUS BRAND ELEMENTS

Let's Roll
MADE IN THE USA
CRUISER
PERFECT MOTORCYCLE STORAGE

WE SHOW MOTORCYCLES
THE RESPECT THEY DESERVE

Let's Roll
MADE IN THE USA
LIFT
PERFECT MOTORCYCLE STORAGE

Let's Roll
MADE IN THE USA
PERFECT MOTORCYCLE STORAGE

Let's Roll
MADE IN THE USA
PERFECT MOTORCYCLE STORAGE

RICH BRAND POOR BRAND PLAYBOOK

Creating a company of giants: FirstSearch, one of Chicago's oldest recruitment firms, thrives by treating candidates and companies as partners, not transactions.

When rebranding them, we cut through the noise of lookalike firms by focusing on their true distinction: eliminating any layers of shallowness and building genuine relationships. Their success comes from being on the same page as clients.

Action tip: Focus on collaboration over competition and align yourself with those you serve. This is how you scale without diluting your values.

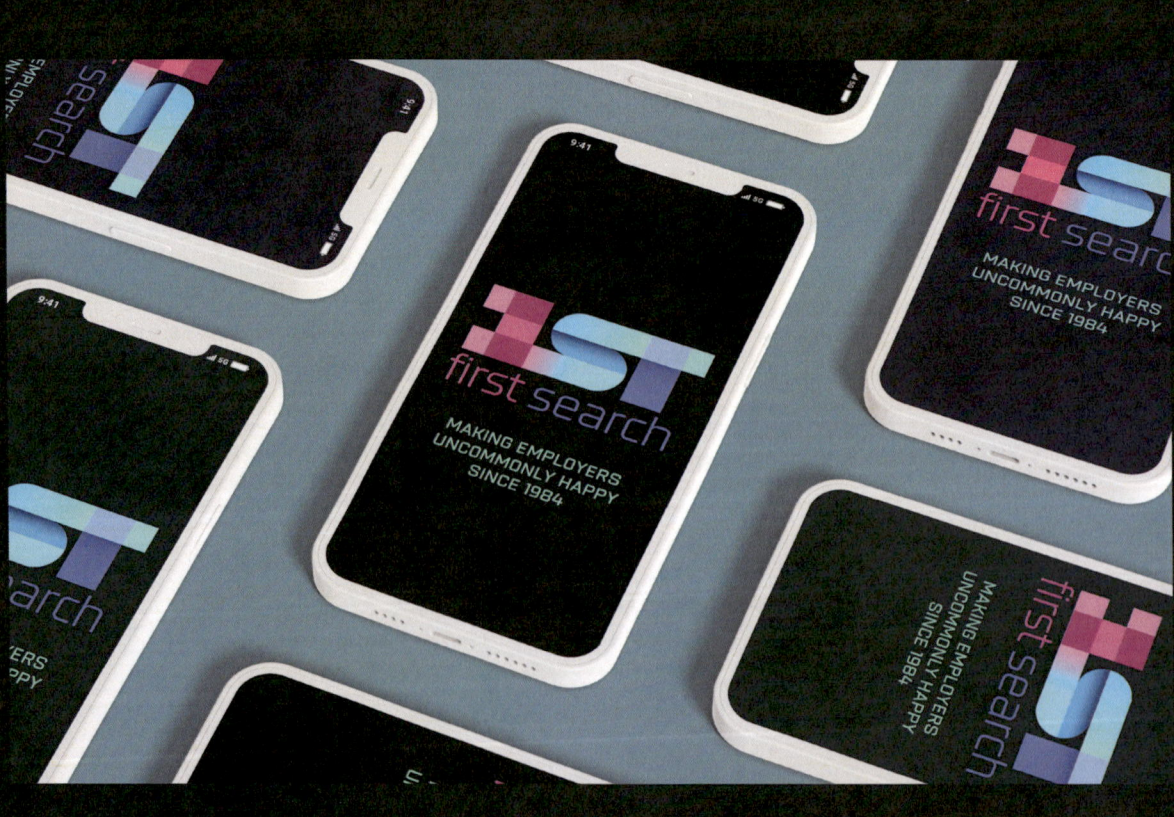

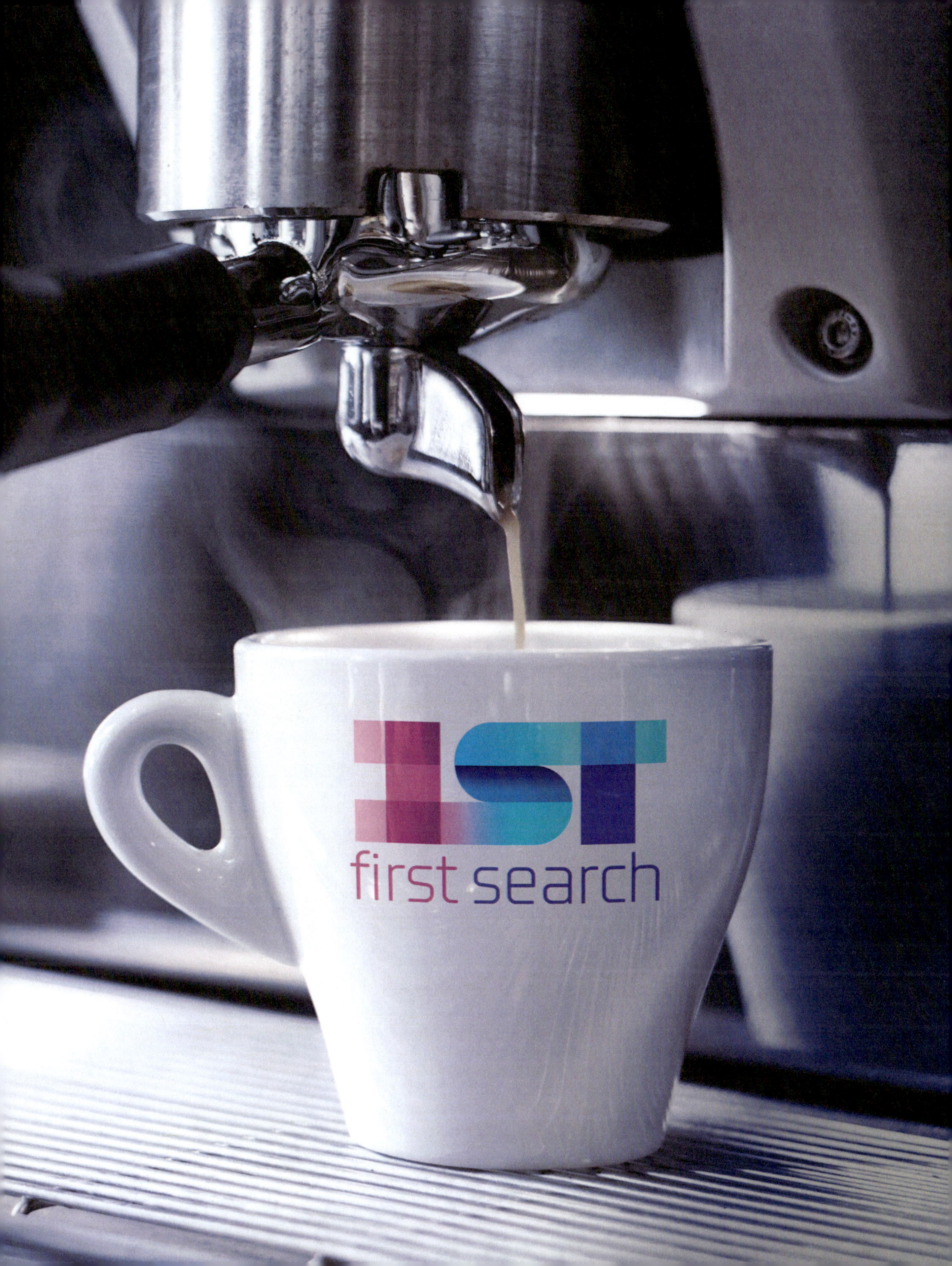
1ST
first search

RICH BRAND POOR BRAND PLAYBOOK

The kind of comfort that kills teams and brands: Money alone is dumb. So why do some individuals outperform others with the same resources? This is why wealth management can get tricky. Especially near retirement when tapping into new opportunities that feel unfamiliar. This is the exact challenge a private investment firm faced.

Our approach? Aligning the firm and its funds with the most established minds in investment history, creating a narrative that educated and empowered clients.

Action tip: Challenge "complacent Goliaths" and encourage people to stop following the herd. How? By becoming the experts through educating (versus selling), and growing together, side by side, with those around you.

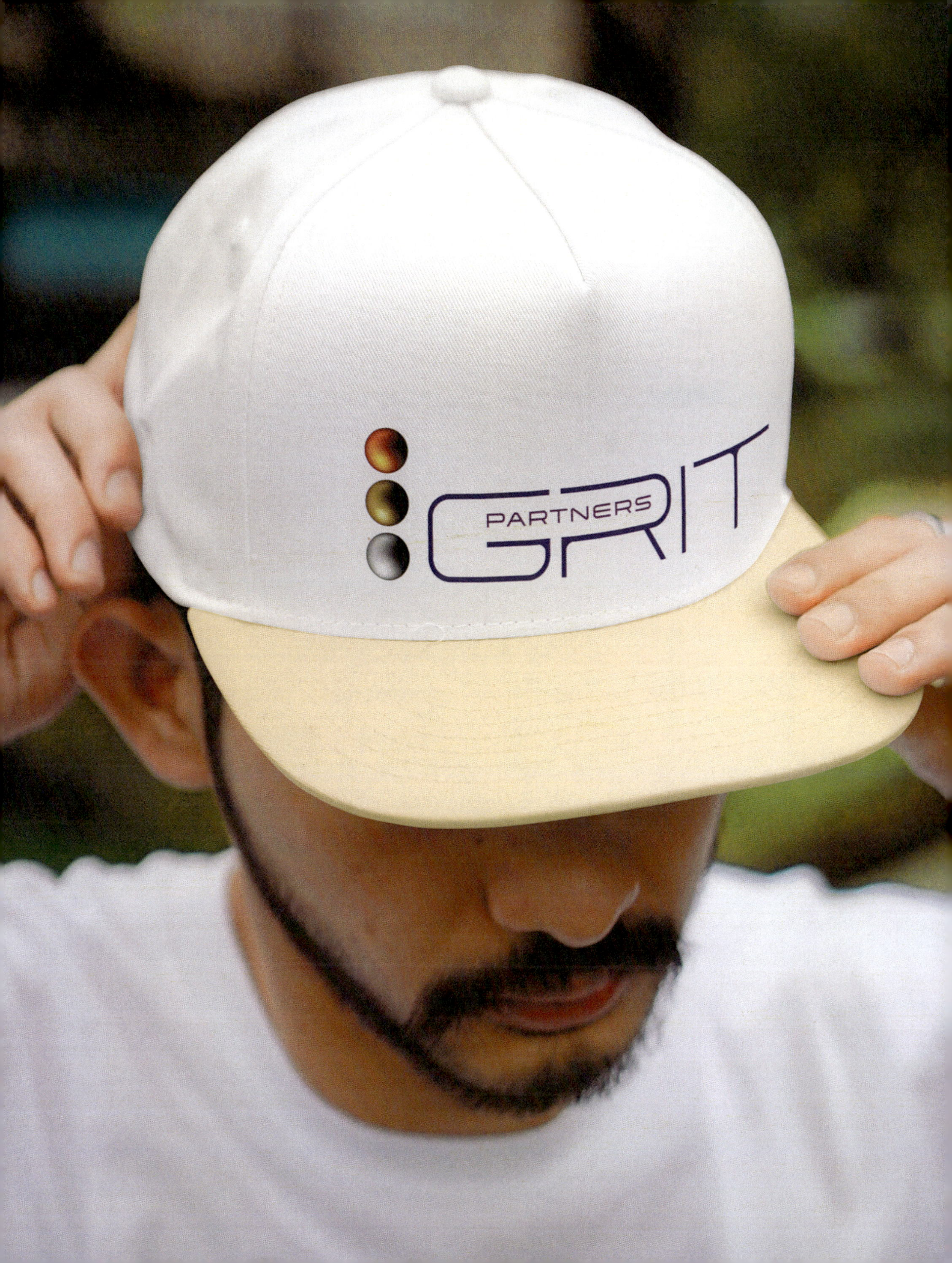
PARTNERS
GRIT

RICH BRAND POOR BRAND PLAYBOOK

Seeing around corners: Businesses are asking the wrong questions. When Dr. David Karli wanted to launch his regenerative therapy clinic, I didn't ask, "How can we look fresh?" Instead, I asked this: "What's our role in the world? What story can we tell that others aren't?"

By blending his medical expertise with these answers, I focused on this critical insight: arthritis affects 22% of American adults, and traditional treatment only masks the problem. This resulted in the tagline, "The Greatest Stride in Joint Self-renewal." Since he was treating the root cause of joint pain, not sedating it.

Action tip: Dig deeper to craft a story rooted in real problems and redefine your industry with it. Safe won't win—disruption will.

KARLI CENTER
THE GREATEST STRIDE IN JOINT SELF-RENEWAL

KARLI CENTER
THE GREATEST STRIDE IN JOINT SELF-RENEWAL

THE GREATEST STRIDE IN JOINT SELF-RENEWAL

KARLI CENTER

KarliCenter.com
MIAMI

SELF RENEW

CELLULAR HEALTH. CELLULAR NUTRITION.
CELLULAR VITALITY.

Fruits & Veggies

Reciprocation: Dental labs all look the same—no distinction, just price wars. When RVDA came to me, I knew we had to break free from the "sea of sameness" drowning the industry.

We didn't just rebrand; we focused on helping dentists to "bond" with their patients. This came to life with a new name, Unbreakable Bonds, and this tagline: "Patients are like teeth. Nobody should lose either of them."

Action tip: Build a brand so unexpected and distinct, it makes the competition irrelevant. Be so bold that it unites your team and your clients.

UNBREAKABLEBONDS.COM

UNBREAKABLE BONDS

PATIENTS ARE LIKE TEETH.
NOBODY SHOULD LOSE
EITHER OF THEM.

The "Taking Small Steps" Myth: In 1936, Alan Turing, the father of modern computing, proved a critical fact: malware can lie dormant indefinitely, undetected. It's been reported 66% of global organizations are susceptible to ransomware, yet "malware solutions" still ignore this.

When COMODO approached us, they had groundbreaking tech with zero breaches and needed to escape the old promises, clichés, and tired claims. So we rebranded them as Xcitium with the slogan: "The Power of Zero. Unleashed."

Action tip: Challenge everyone to stop playing by flawed industry rules. Build a brand that dares to take a bold stand and solve the real problem. The lesson? People don't come to new conclusions with old information.

xcitium

The Power of Zero. Unleashed.

Empowering others: I recently branded a nonprofit aiming to restore dignity and value to America's $30-40 billion sports industry. The problem we were solving: over 70% of US kids drop out of organized sports by age 13. Instead of outdoor fun, they're glued to TikTok.

The solution? A new story and name—True Winners—and a powerful slogan: Bringing sports to life.

Action tip: Challenge your colleagues or clients to stop settling for safe narratives—craft a story bold enough to shift culture and get everyone back in the game.

Bringing sports to life

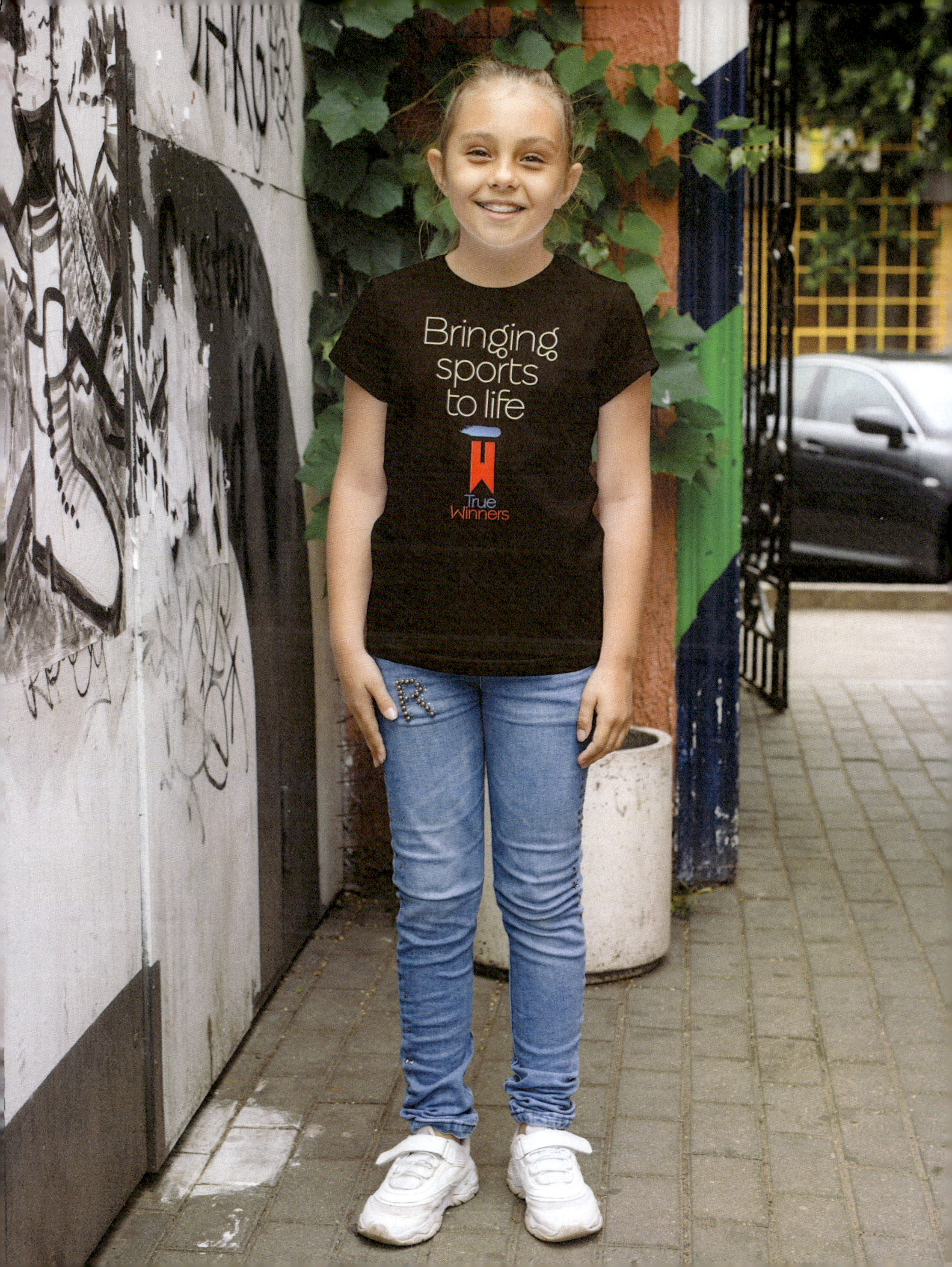
Bringing sports to life
True Winners

Not all differences are the same: Before it became Nimbl Vehicles, the expedition camper company was XP Camper, and everyone had a different vision. The fix? Rallying around one common goal: empowering those who live life on their own terms with zero compromise and a front-row seat to awesome.

That clarity united the team and helped the brand explode into a multi-million-dollar business despite the pandemic.

Action tip: Get your colleagues and clients fighting the same battle. Identify the common enemy and go all-in on defeating it. That's where the real growth lies.

"Herb, I think you've taken this social distancing thing a little too far."
nimbl
FREEDOM TO ROAM
nimblvehicles.com

Empower others: Salesforce is the world's #1 CRM, but small-to-medium businesses had limited options—until StoreConnect stepped in. Built 100% on Salesforce, StoreConnect offered capabilities usually available only to enterprise. The result was more independence and greater options with less stress and hurdles and happier customers.

The CEO, a serial entrepreneur, knew firsthand the pain points SMBs face. Rebranding StoreConnect was simple: focus on empowerment and introduce a new revolution in eCommerce for small-to-medium-sized businesses: Customer Commerce.

Action tip: Become the mirror for those you serve. Reflect their dreams and challenges—and deliver solutions they didn't even know were possible. That's how you stand out.

storeconnect
CUSTOMER COMMERCE

"Doing always beats thinking, the end."

Gary Vaynerchuk

Last word

Here's what's startling: despite empathy and heart being the two greatest assets any company has, you won't find either one on a balance sheet.

Yet, it's the brands with heart that build empires of every size, shape, and color.

They also build communities by becoming the glue that binds us together, uniting our strengths, values, and skills.

Done well, we become unstoppable.

This is why I wrote **Rich Brand Poor Brand**.
It's a reminder and a checklist of what's possible.

History is filled with evidence of how powerful this can be:

Apple began in a basement. Steve Wozniak and Steve Jobs wanted to innovate.

They positioned Apple as a rebel. They challenged the status quo.

Creativity and user-friendly design became their hallmarks.

People around the world rallied to their battle cry.

Coca-Cola isn't just a drink. It's a symbol of unity.

For over 130 years, it's brought people together.

Their Christmas ads are legendary.

Consistent messaging only strengthened their timeless brand story.

Walt Disney dreamed big. He wanted to create magic. Disney's story is about imagination.

It's the power of storytelling in three dimensions.

Nike's journey is about athletic greatness.

"Just Do It" is more than a motto. It's a call to action.

Nike's story is about determination, excellence, and grit. It's about encouraging each of us to push boundaries.

LEGO started in a Danish workshop. It isn't just for kids.

It's proof that unleashing creativity can happen at any age.

Notion aims to simplify work.

Their message is clear and visually appealing.

Notion's story is about making work easier.

Successful brand stories share common traits. They're authentic. They connect emotionally. They highlight unique attributes. They communicate purpose and values clearly.

Craft your brand and its story with these elements.

To connect deeply.

To leave a lasting impression.

To unite your team.

To thrive on ideas and build a team and community that enjoys ingenuity for breakfast, inspiration for dinner, and courage for dessert.

Like I said in the beginning of this book: This is all about unleashing your David in a world of Goliaths.

Now, go and kick some Goliath ass.

Acknowledgments

I am fortunate to have in my circle an amazing group of people who truly have my back.

I will start with my wife Sherry who is my partner in life and living. Thank you for being you, being silly, being smart, and being "my girl." You are my rock who always keeps things in perspective. I am thrilled to have you by my side in life.

Thank you Claude Silver who, day in and day out, displays more heart and care for others in a single hour than anyone I know. Your courage and resilience in believing what's possible is an inspiration to me and anyone lucky enough to know you. I thank you for your enthusiasm, trust, and sheer joy in being part of this project and labor of love.

Thank you to Patricia Ross, my editor, for your enthusiasm, and your trust that, despite my having any apparent roadmap, there is a method to my madness. Claude knows that as "jazz," and you know it as "David."

A big thank you to the one known as "the spicy one." That would be Ronda Taylor who is a kindred spirit and helps bring the book to life. I appreciate your attention to detail, our shared love (and obsession over) fonts, typography, "white space" and all the details that make a project of this nature "rise above the noise." I appreciate you more than you know and thank you for being anything but ordinary.

Thank you to all those I have included in this book.

From Daymond John to Jason Feifer to Sara Blakely to Billy Joel to Phil Knight to Brené Brown to Kevin Hart and Gary Vaynerchuk (and the many who I have not mentioned).

Each of you lights me up. I thank you.

"I'm David."
(Goliath wasn't available for the photo shoot.)

Honest businesses deserve honest help.

I'm David, bestselling author of **Brand Intervention**, the guy Daymond John calls "brilliant with branding," the one Grant Cardone calls "a branding genius," and who Claude Silver calls "a mad creative genius."

Over the past four decades, my work in branding has helped businesses generate in excess of $7 billion worldwide.

You might have seen my work featured in *ADWEEK, Fast Company, Forbes, INC, Huffington Post, Entrepreneur, Thrive Global, the New York Times*, and more. And I've received over 320 international awards, including a rare honor: the Presidential Ambassador for Global Entrepreneurship medallion.

But years ago, I stopped entering industry award shows for a simple reason. I realized that industry shows usually awarded the wrong thing. For me, branding is about differentiation and growth—specifically, helping clients grow. The trophies don't show that.

It's the impact on other people's lives that truly mattered, for example:

To my surprise, Reed Hastings, Netflix co-founder, mentioned me in his bestseller, *No Rules Rules*, alongside Sir Richard Branson and Steve Jobs because of innovation.

That was a moment I won't forget. One of many.

This is why I'm all about helping you achieve what others see as impossible. My passion lies in seeing you grow, reach objectives that seem out of reach, and outsmart industry Goliaths that have gotten complacent. This is where the real fun happens.

If you want to work together, have me as a guest on your podcast, or want me to deliver a keynote speech, don't be shy. Reach out at **david@risingabovethenoise.com**.

Also, join my newsletter. It comes out every Saturday morning and is loaded with insights to help you take on the big players and win. Subscribe to it here: **www.risingabovethenoise.com**.

I want you to have all the knowledge
to build an amazing brand.
Grab the bestseller that started it all:

Grab your copy at Amazon, Barnes and Noble, Books a Million
and anywhere fine books are sold.

Printed in the USA
CPSIA information can be obtained
at www.ICGtesting.com
LVRC092026021224
798134LV00001B/1